Her Session

A One-Act Play

Beth Nahre

ISBN 979-8-89130-186-3 (paperback)
ISBN 979-8-89130-187-0 (digital)

Christian Faith Publishing
832 Park Avenue
Meadville, PA 16335
www.christianfaithpublishing.com

banahre@gmail.com

Printed in the United States of America

Characters

ANNIE BROWN, gregarious, retired teacher with a quirky view of life. She is a widow who is adjusting to life as a widow, and although her friends think she needs help coping, she is sure she is just fine.

KATE STONE, a family counselor with a three-month-old baby at home. She has just gone back to work and is trying to adjust to the challenges of being a working mother.

CHLOE, receptionist, flighty, scattered, ill at ease at her job, but very friendly.

Place

Kate's small office

Time

Late morning on a Monday in January

Her Session

Act One

Scene 1

Lights come up on a small office. A desk is set at angle facing stage left, with a comfortable couch to the right side of the desk. In front of the couch is a coffee table with a box of Kleenex and a vase of real flowers. The desk is neat with a single legal pad, laptop, pencil caddy, two framed pictures, and a baby's pink pacifier. One of the pictures shows herself, husband, and baby, and the other is just the baby. Behind the desk is a bookcase with various books, knickknacks, and smaller pictures. A coat rack is beside the door at stage right. A window is on stage left. KATE, an attractive woman in her midthirties is nervously fidgeting with the various items on her desk, and checking her watch. She picks up her

phone twice and places it back on the desk.
She is neatly dressed in slacks, blouse and
sweater.

KATE *(Walks to the door and opens it).* Please come in, Mrs. Brown. I hope you didn't have trouble getting here in this weather. It was really slick when I left home this morning. I hate driving on ice. *(She directs ANNIE to the couch, where she takes a seat.)* Let me take your coat. I'll just hang it here by the door.

ANNIE. Easier if you want to make a quick getaway…rack close to the door.

KATE. Well, I suppose so. I hope you will want to stay.

ANNIE. Want to stay? Well, I'm here, so I guess I'll give it a shot. But first, I have to tell you, that waiting room of yours is not the kind of place that makes someone feel comfortable about staying.

KATE. Really? Why? I know it's rather drab, but is there something else wrong with it?

ANNIE. It's not the room, it was the other woman *in* the room. From the moment I walked in, she was spilling the details on, I can only assume, her husband. She said, "*It* looks awful. First *it* was purple, then *it* was sort of a green and yellow color, and now *it's* black.

He wouldn't let me touch it. Not that I wanted to touch it, but clearly someone needs to look at it." When they called her into the other office, she turned and added, "I just hope they don't need to cut it off." *(She pauses for breath.)* I know the HIPAA laws are important, but please, what kind of doctor is on the other side of the reception area?

KATE. Oh, Dr. Toreno? She's a podiatrist.

ANNIE. Aah… Foot, toe maybe. Thank God. I was afraid she was a urologist. Well, that's a relief for sure. I think the doctor needs to put a sign out there. I was ready to bolt when she left, and then you opened the door. Good timing on your part.

KATE. I guess Chloe wasn't at the reception desk. I'm so sorry you were upset. Are you alright now? Would tea or a glass of water help?

ANNIE. No. I'm fine. So, here I am. Now what? I've never been to a counselor before. No, wait, that's not true. I did go a couple of times in college. Group therapy. Wow, I learned my life was a piece of cake compared to the other people in that group. Learned a couple of things, became a little more assertive. All and all, I guess it was okay. But counseling, just me and…well, you.

KATE. I see. Why don't you start with explaining why you're here? (*Door opens and CHLOE flies in the door.*)

CHLOE. (*Not noticing the older woman, she interrupts.*) Mrs. Stone, I'm making out the shopping list. Would you rather have hazelnut or vanilla creamer? Dr. Toreno likes hazelnut. I don't like it at all. Well, I don't drink coffee, so I guess it doesn't matter. And Dr. Toreno says to get two-ply instead of one.

KATE. Chloe, I have a client. You shouldn't barge in. We can discuss housekeeping later.

ANNIE. Pumpkin spice is good. Of course, some people only enjoy it around the holidays, but I like the smell of it as much as the taste.

CHLOE. I'm sorry. I guess you came in when I was in the back room.

KATE. It's fine Chloe. Just remember, emergencies only, okay?

CHLOE. No problem. (*She makes a clumsy exit.*)

KATE. I apologize.

ANNIE. No need to apologize. Good help is hard to find. She'll settle in. Just give her some time.

KATE. I'm not sure there's enough time in the world to get her fully functional. (*She realizes she is being less than professional.*) So, let's see, where were we?

ANNIE. Why am I here, you asked? Myra made me come.

KATE. Myra is your daughter?

ANNIE. Myra is my friend. Best friend. But you know how that can be. She is convinced that I can't be "doing so well" since my husband died. Something *must* be wrong with me. So I finally agreed to come just to make *her* feel better. I guess when you're done with me. I should ask for a note to give to Myra. You know, something like, "I have spoken with Ms. Brown, and as a professional, I can attest to the fact that she is, in fact...okey dokey."

KATE. I suppose I could do that, with your permission. So how are you doing?

ANNIE. I hate it when people ask me that! I'm sorry I know that's what you want to know. But when people out there (*gesturing at the door*) want to know, I never know how to answer. Right after my husband died, people would ask, and I always answered, "Right this moment, I'm fine." That's what they wanted to hear. I don't think they really wanted to know that I got so angry one night I knocked everything off his desk, or that I sat on the cold tile floor crying because I couldn't reach the salad spinner on the top shelf of the kitchen cabinet. People want to be polite, so I gave them an answer that would work for them.

KATE. But did it work for you?

ANNIE. Most of the time. And really, I figured if I was angry and sad, that was pretty normal. If I had become a hoarder or wandering around the town square in my bath robe, now that would have been something to be concerned about. I don't know. I just muddled through. No one really wants to see you get too emotional, you know, so it's easier to just nod and smile and…well, you know.

KATE. What about now? How are you really feeling? (*She's interrupted by her phone vibrating on the desktop. She looks at it, and it is obvious she doesn't know what to do.*)

ANNIE. Go ahead, kiddo, answer it. Seriously, take the call. (*Kate is torn between being professional or taking the call.*)

KATE. I shouldn't. This is your time. (*She continues to stare at the phone, reaching for it and pulling her hand back.*)

ANNIE. I promise not to have a breakthrough this very moment. Take the call.

KATE. *(She picks up the phone and turns her back on Annie. Annie leans in to hear better.)* Really? No, she always drops right off after that last morning bottle. Does she have a fever? Is she warm? The thermometer is right there on the changing table. Yes, that's a good idea. Okay. No, it's fine. Yes, or text me. Yes, text me. Thanks Liz. *(she turns back just as Annie leans back into the couch and appears to be examining her nails)* I'm so sorry. This is…

ANNIE. Your first day back at work.

KATE. Is it that obvious?

ANNIE. Well, you seem a little distracted. There's a pacifier on your desk, and I hate to tell you, sweetie, but you have a little bit of spit-up on your back.

KATE. Oh my god. *(She tries to see her back with a tissue in hand but can't reach the spot. Annie takes the tissue from her and lightly dabs at the spot, looks around for the wastebasket, and tosses it in. Kate drops in her chair as Annie goes back to her spot on the couch.)* This is so embarrassing, not to mention unprofessional. I can't imagine what you must be thinking.

ANNIE. I was just remembering my friend Linda. She lived in the duplex next to me when she had her son. She said she picked him up after work and went straight to the store with him. She was in a hurry, and the store smelled bad, and well, it was just one of those crummy days, you know. When she got home, she put the baby down and headed to the bathroom. She looked in the mirror and saw that her little bundle of joy had spit up all over her back, and she had walked all around the store looking like a used burp rag. It wasn't the store that stunk, it was her. What really burned her was that no one told her. So that's what I was thinking. You gotta admit it is pretty funny. (*At this, Kate starts sniffling.*)

KATE. Everyone tried to tell me it wouldn't be like this, you know. You'll be ready to go back. She'll be fine. Lizzie, my babysitter, is really great, I know she is. But I don't know if I'm ready, and I don't know if the baby is fine. But I sure know I'm not doing you any good.

ANNIE. I feel fine, kiddo. Take a breath. Good, now another. Better? I have one word for you: *dryer*.

KATE. What?

ANNIE. Dryer. Do you have a clothes dryer?

KATE. Yes, why do you ask?

ANNIE. Call…Liz, is it? Call Liz and tell her to put…what's your daughter's name?

KATE. Ellie. Her name is Ellie. Eleanor really, but we call her Ellie.

ANNIE. Ellie, cute name. Tell Lizzie to put Ellie in her carrier, pumpkin seat—whatever you mamas call 'em nowadays—put the seat on the dryer, and turn it on. It worked like a charm for my daughter. Sometimes the only naps I got were in the laundry room with my head on a towel, my bottom on the hamper, and my baby up top. Go ahead, call her back. I'm not going anywhere.

KATE. (*She picks up the phone and makes the call.*) Liz, is she still crying? Really? Oh good. Well, if it happens again, put her in her carrier and the carrier on the dryer, and turn it on. Oh sure, it works every time. (*She looks back at Annie and winks.*) Okay, bye. (*She puts phone back on her desk.*) I hope you don't mind I made her think it was my idea. I hate to look like such a rookie in front of her.

ANNIE. Hey, you're part of a big secret mommy group now. We give hints for everything from colic to cradle cap. She had stopped crying, hadn't she? (*Kate nods.*) Yeah, that's the way it goes. How do babies learn so quickly to monopolize your every waking moment and punch

those buttons that feed your insecurity? And just so
you know, it never really ends, the button pushing.

KATE. Well, thank you so much. It's embarrassing to involve
you in my personal life.

ANNIE. Forget it. Ironic, isn't it? I mean, how am I supposed
to be comfortable telling you all about my personal
life and pretend you don't have one? Seems kinda
silly to me. I was a new mother once. My daughter
had a terrible cold, and the doctor gave me these
drops to use. I asked him whether she got two drops
in each nostril or a total of two. He said two drops in
her mouth and looked at me like I was an idiot. How
was I to know? I bet your daughter is, what? Three
months old? That's when moms go back to work. But
it sucks, doesn't it? When you're home, you feel like
you've wasted your education. When you're at work,
you're neglecting your baby. No matter where you
are, you feel like you're missing something and being
judged by everyone. Word of advice, never listen to
Dr. Laura. I've wanted to reach through the radio and
strangle her on more than one occasion. Shaming
women for working when they have children. Women
should support each other, not tear each other down.
Honestly!

KATE. Yes, everybody told me it would be fine. But I really
miss her. I even miss cleaning her up. I miss the way

she smells when she's just had a bath. I like just look-ing at her. *(Pauses, looks away, and then snaps back into professional mode.)* But let's get back to you. Are you sleeping alright, appetite changed, a little on the moody side?

ANNIE. Those are good questions for you, but I know it's my forty-five minutes. I sleep okay, but I hate getting up. Another day, twenty-four hours, and I always think "Well, he's gone," and I don't feel like doing anything alone. I don't recognize my life anymore. I eat, but I don't really enjoy it. I can go from happy and hopeful to miserable and hopeless pretty fast. But again, that's just the way it is. I figure, give me another five to ten years, and I'll forget what I used to feel like. *(Short pause.)* Last week I was making deviled eggs, and I remembered how he used to sit and stare at me when I made them. Just sitting there, looking at me and the eggs with his tongue hanging out. He loved eggs.

KATE. Your husband stared at you when you made deviled eggs?

ANNIE. Oh no. My dog stared at me. I guess I expect you to read my mind, don't I? My dog, not my husband. My dog is gone too. He had to be…well, you know. He was my husband's dog really. He didn't really pay much attention to me unless I was making deviled eggs or taking him for a ride in the car. I remembered that last week, and it make me cry. Deviled eggs. I know it sounds melodramatic, but I feel like I'm on a trip I didn't plan, and I didn't pack correctly and have no idea where I'm going.

KATE. That's a good way of expressing it. You're right about taking a trip you didn't plan, and that would make anyone angry. Do you feel angry?

ANNIE. Sometimes, but not very often. Who would I be angry with? My husband? He didn't plan on taking his trip either. And I'm not angry with me. It's not my fault. I get angry but it passes quickly. I clean when I'm angry and my house isn't a sterile environment, so I guess I've got that covered. You know what it feels like? Remember when you were little and you had the whole summer vacation ahead of you, and the first day, it rains? What are you going to do? All the fun stuff you planned can't happen because of the weather. That's how I feel. I…we had a lot of fun stuff planned, but now I can't do it. I don't want to do it. I'm stuck in the house and the rain just keeps falling.

(The door suddenly opens, and Chloe is standing there with a frightened look on her face.)

CHLOE. I'm sorry, but—

KATE. Chloe, really this has got to stop.

CHLOE. This really is an emergency. I don't know what to do.

KATE. What is the problem, Chloe?

CHLOE. Do I sign for the delivery with my name or your name?

KATE. Well, your name. You're signing that *you* accepted delivery.

CHLOE. Okay, I'll sign then. I guess I'll just put them in the sink in the back room?

KATE. Put what in the sink?

CHLOE. The fish. They're beautiful. Orange, yellow… there's a blue-striped one that's really big. I hope the stopper works in the sink.

KATE. I…we…no, don't sign. We didn't order tropical fish. That's what they are, I guess.

ANNIE. They could be fancy freshwater, but it's doubtful. They look like tangs and clowns, and maybe a trigger.

CHLOE. We didn't? *(A look of realization appears on her face.)* I bet they're supposed to be down the block at that pet store. He got thrown off by our building name.

KATE. Our building is the West Building, how does that confuse anyone?

CHLOE. Well, the pet store is called Ocean View, and if you were in California and viewing the ocean, you would be looking west, right?

ANNIE. Chloe, you make me rethink my feelings about reincarnation.

CHLOE. Why?

ANNIE. Have you ever heard of Gracie Allen?

CHLOE. No, does she work at Ocean View?

KATE. Tell the delivery man to try the pet store, Chloe, and try to stay in the lobby until you see me come out.

(*Chloe leaves.*)

ANNIE. You know, I like her. She doesn't let little setbacks bring her down.

KATE. Again, I'm so sorry. I can see I've got some work to do here, but let's get back to you. So it's direction you need. A goal, a plan, something to move toward?

ANNIE. Or a different climate. Yeah. That sounds about right. Myra wants me to be happier, seem happier. I'm just glad not to feel worse. I'm stuck somewhere in the middle. That's where I am, in the middle.

KATE. Everything you're stating is perfectly normal, and you're expressing it very well. It's not unusual to feel somewhat lost or adrift after losing your spouse. Your life took a 180-degree turn. It can be very disorienting and confusing. What I'm saying is, it's okay to be angry, confused, and sad.

ANNIE *(nodding)*. These things I know. I hate waking up, and there's a whole day ahead. Sometimes the only person I talk to all day is the poor teenager in the drive-through. It's hard to build your day around that. Although I really was thinking of asking her how she got her hair that color—it was turquoise. TV is a distraction. The funny shows *we* used to enjoy aren't fun to watch alone. I can't stand to watch the news. Everyone's angry and blaming everyone else. I do have one guilty TV pleasure *(seems embarrassed)*. I love the *Real Housewife* shows. Isn't that awful? They're awful, always fighting and complaining about some stupid thing. Of course they complain in their 3.2-million-dollar homes or in their chauffeur-driven limos. I yell at them out loud. I tell myself it's therapeutic. It feels therapeutic. It feels like I'm playing a part in someone else's life. This is not my life. This is not what

I was expecting. This is not fair *(pause for ten-count)*. And that's when it gets bad. You know, *bad*.

KATE. It's traumatic, it's real, and your grief won't look exactly like anyone else's grief. There's no "doing it right." It's a process that you will work on for the rest of your life. You don't have to fix everything today or tomorrow or this year. You decide what you want, and maybe I can help you find a way to get it. Everything you've just expressed is common, but that's not a comfort is it? You want to feel better, happier. You want to feel like yourself again. So you have to stop and ask yourself what makes you happy? You're allowed to be selfish. Give yourself a gift. What do you want? Where do you want to be? Who do you like being with? These are all questions you need to answer honestly, and from there, you can make plans for a new future.

ANNE. You make it sound…possible. It's hard for me to think about those things when he's not here. I feel unfaithful trying to be happy, thinking of just me.

KATE. And what would he say? Would he like you to be mourning forever, or enjoying your life?

ANNE. He would say "Get on with it. Get going. Move!"

KATE. Sounds like a good man. *(Annie nods quietly.)* So do you think your friends really know how you feel? Or do you keep them in the dark for the most part?

ANNIE. Sometimes I'm real. But it just makes people uncomfortable. I feel better when everybody else is happy. People-pleaser, shift the attention—that's what I do. So I don't share the really bad stuff.

KATE. What stuff would that be? *(The phone rings.)* What is it? *(Harshly spoken.)* Panicky, she sounds panicky? Put her through. What is it, Mother? Is Dad alright? Uh-huh. Yes, yes, that's to be expected. Well, you say he took a long walk? Uh huh. Yes, it's fine. He's not in any pain, is he? Well, of course he's winded, he just took a long walk. What's he doing now? Good. That's good. It's okay, Mother, I know. Don't worry. Well, I know, we both worry, don't we? It's okay. I'll call you after work, okay? Good. Love you too. *(Pause.)* My mother. Dad had a mild heart attack three months ago. She hovers over him like a hawk. He took a walk, and when he got home, he was tired. She needs a lot a reassuring. Again, I'm so sorry. I don't think you're getting your best shot with me.

ANNIE. I don't agree. It lets me see what kind of person you are. You care. I would rather have a counselor who cares than one who is only efficient.

KATE. So you were about to tell me about the really bad stuff. What's that like?

ANNIE. The moments of complete hopelessness and fear that this is it…until I'm gone. That everyone else has a plan, a purpose, a goal. And most of them are sharing those with someone else. Even sharing problems is sharing. Should I get a new roof, should I fix the car or trade it in? I have to figure it out. I don't like figuring things out by myself. So no real plan, just "Pay this bill, do that thing." I don't have any real goals or plans beyond hanging on. I'm in limbo. I can't go on. All my plans were meant to be shared, and if it's just me, what's the point?

KATE. There are a lot of plans that you could make that could involve other people even if they're not there planning with you. Sounds like you followed other people's plans for most of your life.

ANNIE. Happily. You know my husband and I raised our daughter to be self-sufficient, independent, you know? And dammit, she is. Well, she asks my opinion sometimes, and I ask for hers. But we both know there are boundaries. I'm glad we are honest with each other. She's grieving too after all. We help each other, but she goes home to her husband and children, which is good, and I just go home. So I liked following my husband's lead. He was a good leader I happily followed.

KATE. Granted, happily, but you're capable of being in charge. You can choose. I can help you look at your possibilities—how you connect with people, how you bring them into your plan. You decide. You choose.

ANNIE. Oooh. That sounds like me making secret plans to invade other people's lives. (*Just then there is a loud banging noise. She is startled. Kate shows no reaction.*) You don't suppose Chloe just used a crow bar on the copy machine, do you?

KATE. It's the furnace. Wait…there will be two more thunks.

(*Sound is repeated. Ten seconds of silence, and then the final bang.*)

ANNIE. Does your landlord know about that? Geez. I'm guessing someone in really bad shape might just pee. (*Eyes the couch.*) Aah, hence the faux leather couch. (*Slight pause.*) I'm guessing you get at least of few of those, right? People really going off the rail.

KATE (*ignoring her question*). Oh, believe me the landlord knows about the five-hundred-year-old furnace. Dr. Toreno and I own the building.

ANNIE. Really? Huh, well, good for you, running your own show.

KATE. This show may close if we don't get more clients and patients in her. Oh, I'm sorry. This is not the time or the place to…I've really done a bang-up job with you today, getting off course. I hope you'll forgive me for being so unprofessional.

ANNIE. I don't mean to make you feel worse, but I'm not exactly standing out on a ledge somewhere. *(She stands and walks to the window and looks out.)* Which is good because there really aren't any good jumping off spaces around here. Besides I like talking to you. You're a real person, not just a health-care provider with one eye on the clock. So, the whole building? What's in the back?

KATE. No fish tank, that's for sure. Oh, four more offices and two bathrooms. You did it again. You got me off track.

ANNIE. *(She walks to the desk.)* Can I use that pad? *(As she reaches for the pad, she knocks the pencil caddy off the desk. Kate gets up to retrieve it as Anne slips into her chair and picks up the one pencil that is left on the desk.)* You know, you could really make this work better if you made just a few changes. First, that lobby. Ugh. Put Chloe at the far end. That way, she has time to think as she walks across the room. Some art on the walls, bright cheery colors. And you know, a fish tank can be quite relaxing. I've got a thirty-gallon fish tank in my shed and all the pumps and hoses. *(She stops for a moment to think.)* Does Dr. Toreno have any kids?

KATE. Yeah, she has a two-year-old daughter, Clara.

ANNIE. Where is Clara when Dr. Toreno is here?

KATE. Oh, she's with the nanny at home. Why?

ANNIE. It just seems silly to me to have two nannies with two babies and two moms who miss their babies. Why not take one of the offices and make it into a play-room-combination-nursery, put one nanny there, and the other in the reception room. Or maybe Chloe would be better with the kiddos, and the nannies could job-share the reception job? Then you could see your kids, they could see you, your stress level goes down, and you have a built-in nanny if either one of yours gets sick. See? The nannies could switch back and forth day to day, hour to hour. They get some control over their hours at work. People like having a say in their schedule. It might cost you a little more money.

KATE. Well, yes. More money, I don't know—we're pretty tight right now. But that maybe could work.

ANNIE. And I know a woman, Charlene, who is a traveling masseuse. She could rent the other office and bring in a little rent. You know, you could make it worth her while. You could call it a…"women helping women" discount on the rent until it catches on. Maybe add a stylist—ooh, or a day spa. Of course, that's something for the future, but there isn't anything like that around here.

KATE. I don't know… A masseuse? That sounds a little like…well, you know.

ANNIE. Charlene's a trained therapist, and she doesn't charge by the hour. And there's no pole involved. She's really good. I've gone to her a few times, and I said I would never have a massage. But boy, howdy, did I change my mind. It was wonderful. Some of your patients could use a little stress reduction. I'm just guessing, of course. *(She starts making notes on the pad as she continues talking.)* If you crossmarketed it right with a new name for the building, a logo, some publicity, public service of some kind, and did the work yourself, except for the furnace, I think this could be a great place of healing. Does your husband have any handy skills? Do you have a husband?

KATE. I do have a husband, and he's more handy on the computer, but he's a fast learner. It sounds great Annie, but I don't have time to do all that and work and take care of the baby and Jason. No, let's get back to you. This is your time, your session, not mine.

ANNIE. You're right. It is my session, and I feel great. Don't you get it? I can do all the running around, figuring stuff out, looking for grant money, measuring. All that stuff that you don't have time to do. I have plenty of time. And best of all, I'm very affordable… I'd do it for free counseling, as needed, or when Myra thinks I need a tune-up. Don't you see? This is just what I needed—a plan, a goal, people planning with me. This could solve all our problems, issues, whatever. What do you think?

KATE. I have to admit, it sounds wonderful. Somehow this all seems slightly weird—you, me, this idea. This is not the way I imagined my day going. I'm not sure everyone would find it professional.

(The door opens. Chloe rushes in.)

CHLOE. The mail's here. I know it's not an emergency, but you may be a finalist in the Publisher's Clearing House contest!

KATE. Chloe, have you done any babysitting?

CHLOE. Are you kidding? I have five younger brothers and a baby sister.

KATE *(speaking to Annie)*. Maybe being professional can also mean creative problem-solving. *(Speaking to Chloe.)* Chloe, can you stay after for just a few moments?

CHLOE. Sure, Mrs. Stone. My dog obedience class was called off because Janie has fleas.

KATE. I'm afraid to ask.

ANNIE. This is great, isn't it? And you're probably a little worried. Honestly, you don't know me from Adam. I'm honest and trustworthy. But I could give you references. Which I should. You need to know I'm on the level. Why don't you think about it? Talk to Jason and Dr. Toreno, and I'll talk to Charlene and get my resumé together. *(She gets up and walks to the coat rack and puts on her coat.)* I have to tell you Kate this has been a great session. I feel ten years younger. I'm going to take myself out to lunch, and I'm going to order dessert. Women's Health Center, Healing Center, Women's Healing Center, Women Healing Women, yeah that sounds good. Oh *(she opens her purse and starts rummaging through it),* you'll take a check, won't you?

KATE. That would be fine. *(She glances at her watch seeming somewhat puzzled that Annie is leaving.)*

ANNIE. That's one hundred…ten, right? *(She rips up a pre-written check out of her book.)*

KATE *(still somewhat confused)*. Yes.

ANNIE *(slight pause)*. You need to charge more if you want people to take you seriously. I'll be back on Friday with a full report, okay? Give me an appointment at one o'clock, if it's open. If not, give me a call, Chloe, my number's on the check. Thank you, Kate. Myra was right. I needed to come here and talk to you. You're great! Give Ellie a kiss from her Aunt Annie. See you Friday! *(She opens the reception room door and pauses as she speaks to someone in the lobby area.)* Oh, this is your husband? Did they cut it off?

(Curtains.)

About the Author

Beth Nahre grew up in Muncie, Indiana. She decided at a young age to become a teacher and graduated with her teaching degree from Ball State University. Moving to southern Indiana with her husband, she became part of the Shelbyville community, raising her daughter, teaching fifth- and sixth-grade students, being part of a local writing group, and participating in theater. After her daughter married and she and her husband retired, she became a widow when her husband suddenly died. Two years later, she moved back to Muncie to be close to her daughter, son-in-law, and grandchildren. Enjoying being an assistant director on a one-act play, she decided to try her hand at writing a play that would help her adjust to her new home, new struggles, and the new normal. And so, *Her Session* was written.